Date _____

This book belongs to

_____

Given by _____

Living the
10 Commandments
for Children

Rosemarie Gortler & Donna Piscitelli
Illustrated by Mimi Sternhagen

Our Sunday Visitor Publishing Division
Our Sunday Visitor, Inc.
Huntington, Indiana 46750

Nihil Obstat
Rev. Cornelius O'Brien
Censor Deputatus

Imprimatur
Rev. Frank J. Ready, V.G.
Diocese of Arlington
June 20, 2006

The *Nihil Obstat* and *Imprimatur* are official declarations that a book is free from doctrinal or moral error. It is not implied that those who have granted the *Nihil Obstat* and *Imprimatur* agree with the contents, opinions, or statements expressed.

Scripture citations are from the *Catholic Edition of the Revised Standard Version of the Bible* (RSV), copyright © 1965 and 1966 by the Division of Christian Education of the National Council of the Churches of Christ in the United States of America, and the *Catholic Edition of the New Revised Standard Version of the Bible* (NRSV), copyright © 1989 and 1993 by the Division of Christian Education of the National Council of the Churches of Christ in the United States of America; used by permission; all rights reserved. The wording of the Ten Commandments is from pages 496 and 497 of the English translation of the *Catechism of the Catholic Church* for the United States of America copyright © 1994, United States Catholic Conference, Inc. — Libreria Editrice Vaticana. English translation of the *Catechism of the Catholic Church: Modifications from the Editio Typica* copyright © 1997, United States Catholic Conference, Inc. — Libreria Editrice Vaticana.

Every reasonable effort has been made to determine copyright holders of excerpted materials and to secure permissions as needed. If any copyrighted materials have been inadvertently used in this work without proper credit being given in one form or another, please notify Our Sunday Visitor in writing so that future printings of this work may be corrected accordingly.

Our Sunday Visitor Publishing Division
Our Sunday Visitor, Inc.
200 Noll Plaza
Huntington, IN 46750

ISBN: 978-1-59276-231-6 (Inventory No. T282)

Cover design by Monica Haneline
Cover and interior art by Mimi Sternhagen
Interior design by Sherri L. Hoffman

PRINTED IN CHINA

Contents

A Letter From the Authors

Dear Children,

A very long time ago, God talked to a man named Abraham. God promised that He would be our God, and that we would be His people.

God made us, and He loves us. God really, really wants us to love Him. And He also wants us to love and take care of one another.

To help us become the best people we can be, God carved His Ten Commandments in stone and gave them to Moses to teach us. When we love and praise God, we become strong enough to follow these rules. The more we love and praise God, the better we follow the commandments and show others to do that, too.

Many years later, God sent His Son, Jesus. Jesus lived His life *showing us* how to live these commandments.

To live these commandments means that we sometimes have to resist *temptation* and do the right thing. Temptation is that strong feeling to do something that is wrong. But living the commandments makes us healthier, happier, and at peace with God and one another. And that's a great feeling!

God bless you.

Rosemarie and Donna

First Commandment

**I AM THE LORD YOUR GOD:
YOU SHALL NOT HAVE STRANGE GODS
BEFORE ME.**

Just what are strange gods?
    Are they funny-looking gods,
        like aliens from another planet?
        Or make-believe,
            like cartoons?

Not at all!

Our God tells us
    He is the only
        real and true God!

But sometimes we act as if a person or a thing
is as important as God,
    like when we skip Mass to see a ball game
        or when we treat others badly
        because we want a certain videogame
            or even a special cookie!
Then, that ball game or that videogame
    or that cookie has become a strange god
        because we've made it so important
            that we've done something bad to get it.

FOR
THE
POOR

We don't want *anything* or *anyone*
   to be so important that we do bad things.
      We don't want strange gods!

And …
   if a person thinks a lot of money is the
      most important thing in life,
      and never helps the needy — that's not right.

God knows we need money to buy what
   we need, and sometimes what we want.
      But when a person loves money
         and is selfish,
            then money is a strange god, too!

Let's keep God first in our lives.
How?
By remembering that God loves us and made us.

Loving Him,
   and living the way He teaches us to live,
      must be the most important thing in our lives.

For us there is one God, the Father, from whom
are all things and for whom we exist.
(1 Corinthians 8:6 – RSV)

Second Commandment

YOU SHALL NOT TAKE THE NAME OF THE LORD YOUR GOD IN VAIN.

The name of God is very, very holy.

Sometimes when people are angry
    they forget this.

They use God's name profanely ("in vain").
    That means
        they use God's name as a curse word.

This commandment says we must not do that!

We wouldn't want our own name
    to be used as a curse word, either.
That would really hurt our feelings.

And sometimes people curse in other ways.
    They ask God to hurt somebody.

God wouldn't do that!
    He loves every person,
        and every person is His friend.

We would not want someone
    to ask us
        to hurt our friend.

That would be terrible.
    God wants us to see goodness in other people
        and to be fair and forgiving —
            just as Jesus was when He lived on earth.

Besides …
profane words
    and curse words and words that hurt others
        make people look
            and sound ugly.

God tells us to use His name
    with love,
        gratitude,
           and reverence.

This is how we obey the Second Commandment.

"And blessed is [your] glorious, holy name and
to be highly praised and highly exalted for ever."
(Daniel 3:30 – RSV)

16

Third Commandment

REMEMBER TO KEEP HOLY
THE LORD'S DAY.

What is the "Lord's Day"?
The Lord's Day is the day the Lord rested.

He created the world in six days
    and rested on the seventh day.

God gave us six days to work,
and told *us* to rest
    and to praise Him
        on the seventh day.

This day of rest and praise
    is called the Lord's Day (or the Sabbath).

Since the time of the early Christians,
    the Lord's Day has been celebrated on Sundays —
        but even if you go to Mass on Saturday evening,
        that's considered a Sunday Mass.

Why is the Lord's Day on Sunday?
Because that is the day Jesus rose from the dead.

So how should we keep it holy?
    Well, Jesus showed us how.

Jesus prayed often,
     by talking to God, His Father.
Did you know that
     talking to God is prayer?

Jesus taught and prayed often
     in the synagogue.
A synagogue is the Jewish place of worship,
     just as the church is the place
          we go for Mass.

We can keep the Third Commandment
     by going to Mass,
          praying a little extra,
               and spending time with family.

Keeping the Lord's Day holy
     praises and honors God.
What a great way to thank God
     for all His gifts!

"The sabbath was made for man,
not man for the sabbath; so the Son of man
     is lord even of the sabbath."
          (Mark 2:27 – RSV)

Fourth Commandment

**HONOR YOUR FATHER
AND YOUR MOTHER.**

This commandment is very simple.

God wants us to love
      and respect
            our parents.

God gave us parents
      to love us
            and care for us.

Our parents might be
      natural parents.
Or they might have adopted us.
Some children are raised by grandparents,
      and some have foster parents.
            Jesus had a foster father — Saint Joseph.

This commandment also means we honor
      other people who care for us,
            like teachers, police officers,
                  priests, and nuns.

So God wants us to respect
 our parents.

Jesus always obeyed Mary, His Mother,
 Joseph, His foster father,
  and God, His Father.

Remember when Mary and Joseph
 thought Jesus was lost?
When they found Him
  and asked Him to come home,
   He went with them
    and was obedient to them.

Amazing!
Jesus is God,
 and He obeyed two human parents!

The Fourth Commandment tells us
 to honor and obey our parents.

We thank God, who gave us life.
We thank our parents, who cooperated with God
 to give us life.

And he went down with them and came
to Nazareth, and was obedient to them.
(Luke 2:51 – RSV)

24

Fifth Commandment

YOU SHALL NOT KILL.

Doesn't everybody know this?

Well … think about the times
    when we watch TV shows
        and movies
            that are violent.

Sometimes, TV and movies
    make violence look cool.

Some people call this entertainment.

It really isn't.
Watching a lot of violence
    slowly teaches us
        not to care very much about other people.

And guess what?
    We don't even realize
        we are learning to be hard-hearted
            and uncaring.

The Fifth Commandment also tells us
    to walk away
        from fights when possible
            and to avoid hurting
                other people's feelings.

We can hurt others
    when we call them names
        or ignore them
            or refuse to be their friend.

God wants us to care
    for ourselves
        and for our neighbors.

Jesus showed us how to live this commandment.
    He was always good to other people.

All life is a gift from God.
    Life is special!
        Life is holy!

"I say to you that every one who is angry with his
brother shall be liable to judgment; whoever insults
his brother shall be liable to the council."
(Matthew 5:22 – RSV)

Sixth Commandment

YOU SHALL NOT COMMIT ADULTERY.

God blesses marriage
between a man and a woman.
When two people get married
God gives them to each other.
This is very special!
They would not want to go out
and get somebody else!

God blesses the single life, too!
Many very special and holy people
live single lives.

Some live religious lives.
Others live single lives in the world.
This is also very special.

Whether married or single,
God wants us to respect one another
and ourselves.

He wants us to keep ourselves pure.

30

What does it mean to stay pure?

Well …
    we respect other people
        by treating them with dignity.

We respect ourselves
    by respecting our bodies and the bodies of others.

We wear clothing that covers our bodies well,
    and we make good entertainment decisions.
We choose TV shows,
        movies, magazines, and games
that are clean and wholesome.

We make choices that don't offend God,
    and that don't tempt us
        to be impure.

God shows us how to love one another
    by the way He loves us.
A very holy love is the love of husband and wife —
    the same love that God has for us.

Beloved, we are God's children now....
And all who have this hope in him purify
themselves, just as he is pure.
(1 John 3:2-3 – NRSV)

32

Seventh Commandment

YOU SHALL NOT STEAL.

Is it OK to take that toy?
    It's such a small thing,
        and no one will ever know.

But God will know.
And it offends Him when we take something
    that doesn't belong to us.

This commandment says:
What other people have belongs to them,
    no matter how big
        or small it is.
If it isn't yours,
    don't take it.

What if your sister
    took something of yours?
Isn't it OK to take something of hers,
    just to get her back?

Nope.
It not only hurts the person we take from …
    it also offends God when we steal.

Do you know what else
    this commandment means?
It means we should not talk
    about other people in a bad way.

Yup! Gossip steals a person's reputation.

How do you steal a reputation?
Well … you know what it feels like
    to have someone say something
        bad about you
            behind your back?
It hurts a lot!

What if people believe
    what they are told about you,
        even if it is untrue?
Well, then someone took away
    your reputation!

God wants us to love one another.
God tells us to keep the Seventh Commandment.
    This is how we love one another,
        and love God.

"No servant can serve two masters....
You cannot serve God and [money]."
(Luke 16:13 – RSV)

36

Eighth Commandment

YOU SHALL NOT BEAR FALSE WITNESS
AGAINST YOUR NEIGHBOR.

What does this mean?
Well … bearing false witness
    is the same thing as
        telling a lie.

This commandment says
    God does not want us
        to tell lies.

What if you tell
    just a little,
        tiny lie?
Big or small,
        telling lies is wrong.

What if the lie is told
    to make someone feel better?

Well, that person might feel better
    for a little while.
But how will they feel when they find out
    you told a lie?
How do you feel when you know
    you are lying?

You see,
    telling a lie
        does not help anyone.

But it does offend God,
    who loves you so much!

What if you tell a lie to cover your mistake?
    It might keep you out of trouble, for a while.
        But telling a lie never really
            covers up our mistakes,
because then we have to tell more lies
    to cover the first lie.

So telling a lie never helps us.
It hurts us,
    and it offends God.

Even if we *think* we can get away with a lie,
    God is always with us.
        He hears us.
God's Eighth Commandment
    tells us to be truthful.

"He committed no sin, and no deceit
was found in his mouth."
(1 Peter 2:22 – NRSV)

Ninth and Tenth
Commandments

**YOU SHALL NOT COVET YOUR NEIGHBOR'S WIFE.
YOU SHALL NOT COVET YOUR NEIGHBOR'S GOODS.**

What does it mean "to covet"?

Well …
to covet something is to
really, really want something
that somebody else has.

Remember the Sixth Commandment
and how God says we must keep ourselves pure,
whether single or married?

And remember the Seventh Commandment?
In that one, God told us not to steal.

Well …
the Ninth and Tenth Commandments tell us
to guard the way we want things
that other people have.

These commandments tell us to avoid temptation,
that strong feeling to do something that is wrong.

Everybody has temptations.
    And God knows this!
And God knows how strong
    temptations are!

But He tells us to
    resist temptation,
        whether it is for somebody else's
            husband or wife
                or for somebody else's belongings.

He wants us to find joy
    in the gifts He has given *us*.

And guess what?
    He wants us to be happy
        for the gifts He gives to others, too!

How often do we thank God
    for the gifts He gives to other people —
        especially when we want that gift?

This is a hard thing to do!
    It is called being unselfish,
        and *being unselfish*
            is a very holy thing to do.

Imagine how this would make God smile!

God gives each of us what we need.
    But this is not always the same
        as what we want.

God knows what is best for us.

And you know what?
    Sometimes we don't even recognize
        all the gifts and talents
            God has given us.

God wants us to be grateful for all His gifts.
The Ninth and Tenth Commandments tell us
    to avoid the temptation of
        coveting what other people have.

I appeal to you therefore, brothers and sisters, by
the mercies of God, to present your bodies as a
living sacrifice, holy and acceptable to God.
(Romans 12:1 – NRSV)

For Family Discussion

Why do we need traffic lights on busy streets?

Why do you need a license to drive a car or fly a plane?

Why can't a storekeeper sell beer to a 15-year-old?

Because these are our laws! Laws are rules that are meant to protect us.

Sometimes we find rules uncomfortable and binding. But there is safety in knowing, and following, rules. And when we choose to break the rules, we usually regret it, wishing we had done the right thing.

God's rules — the Ten Commandments — are intended to protect us and to keep us safe and healthy. Because God knows best, and He wants us to be with Him for all eternity, He gave us these rules. They tell us how to resist temptations, which would eventually hurt us.

Temptations are all around us — and they are tricky!

Please check out some Tricky Temptations online at www.osv.com — go to "BOOKS" and select "Book Resources and Downloads." We hope your family will have lively discussions about them. Have fun discussing them — and watch out for those Tricky Temptations!

About the Authors

Rosemarie Gortler is an R.N. and a licensed professional counselor. She is also a eucharistic minister, a member of the Secular Franciscan Order, and a volunteer for Project Rachel. Rosemarie and her husband, Fred, have five children and eighteen grandchildren.

Donna Piscitelli is a school administrator in Fairfax, Virginia. She is active in her church and in Christian outreach. She and her husband, Stephen, have four children and nine grandchildren.

Mimi Sternhagen is a home-school teacher and mother of five children. She and her husband, Don, assist with Family Life ministry in their parish. In addition to her collaborated works with Rosemarie and Donna, Mimi has illustrated *Catholic Cardlinks: Patron Saints*, and *Teach Me About Mary*.

The authors extend their gratitude to Father Donald Rooney of St. Mary's Catholic Church in Fredericksburg, Virginia, and Father Francis De Rosa of St. Louis Catholic Church in Alexandria, Virginia, for their assistance in the preparation of this book.

Other books in this series include:
Little Acts of Grace
Just Like Mary
The Mass Book for Children